Slightly
Famous People's Foxes

Run to earth by

Oliver Pritchett

The gallery of vulpine characters on the following pages have been contributed by friends of *Slightly Foxed* to celebrate the magazine's tenth anniversary. All profits from the sale of this book will be donated to the Children's Hospital School at Great Ormond Street, which enables children to continue their education while they are there. The money will go to buy books to read for pleasure, which can mean so much to children who are away from home, sometimes in isolation or undergoing long and painful treatments.

Slightly Foxed would like to thank the following for contributing their time and expertise gratis: Oliver Pritchett; B. Lodge; Smith Settle Ltd and MK Graphics, both of Yeadon, West Yorkshire.

ISBN 978-1-906562-61-8

Published by
Slightly Foxed Limited
53 Hoxton Square
London N1 6PB

tel 020 7033 0258
www.foxedquarterly.com

Printed and bound by Smith Settle, Yeadon, West Yorkshire

Contents

CONTENTS

Introducing the Literary Fox

Foxes have lived with us in our towns and cities for so long that they must surely have absorbed a good deal of our culture. I actually believe there is now a substantial population of bookish foxes. These are the ones who have ripped open the plastic bags outside publishers' offices and, in the early hours, strewn literary agents' rubbish across the pavement. Some have lairs under the garages of many of our great authors and poets, and come out at night to pore over first drafts that have been binned. Others lurk outside publishers' launch parties, eavesdropping on the literary chatter and the barks of laughter, waiting for the leftover canapés to be chucked out with the empty bottles.

Sometimes I look out of my window at two in the morning and see a nonchalant vixen trotting down the middle of the street, and I guess she is returning from a meeting of a foxes' reading group where they have been chewing over William Boyd's latest, or the new Alice Munro. Refreshments will have been served – possibly a rather pleasing crust of discarded *Quattro stagioni* pizza. That sudden rasping bark in the middle of the night could easily be a dog fox literary critic expressing a harsh opinion, and those yelps the excitable cubs play-fighting over a tattered John Grisham paperback.

No doubt some foxes occasionally grow tired of city life – it all seems so superficial, seeing the same old fox faces at the same old wheelie bins. They yearn to get away from it all to a simple existence in the country, living off the land and perhaps writing the Great Novel. But then they worry, where would the stimulus be? All they'd have for company would be a few squawking, panic-stricken chickens and a lot of dim rabbits. To be honest, they would miss the literary gossip.

The thought of rural crime is also off-putting – all those gamekeepers with shotguns, all those characters in pink coats loitering on horseback in woodland corners, uttering strange, harsh cries. They have also heard stories of hooligan hounds going round in noisy packs. This sort of coarseness causes distress to the sensibilities of the foxes in Bloomsbury and other bookish places such as Hay-on-Wye.

The countryside may be all right for creatures who were born there, but the average urban fox knows it's not really his scene. There's something about being out in the street just before dawn and catching that unmistakable sour smell that tells you a man has been in the neighbourhood. Humans have their faults; certainly no fox is going to get sentimental about them, but it is somehow good to know they are around.

Indeed it wouldn't surprise me if some of the more artistically inclined members of the urban fox population are not, at this very moment, crouched in their lairs with scraps of waste paper, having a go at drawing sketches of various famous human beings.

OLIVER PRITCHETT

A fox in a Barbour and posh Hunter wellies – this could easily be a new member of Posy Simmonds's wonderful cast of cartoon characters, along with Tamara Drewe, Gemma Bovery, George and Wendy Weber, smoothie Stanhope and the rest. He's obviously a bounder, up to no good and sniffing out some dodgy possibilities. We guess he's often to be found in a corner of the saloon bar in the village pub and we suspect his name is Guy – or possibly Piers.

Tracy Chevalier

With a cunning which is typical of the species, the fox dreamed up by the novelist Tracy Chevalier has disguised itself as a Siamese cat. It plans to insinuate itself into the house of a cat-loving family, live on a rich diet of meaty chunks, and snooze on its mistress's lap while attempting to give a convincing impression of a purr. The only flaw in the fox's masterplan is that oversized tail, which may lead to its unmasking.

This creature is known as the 'urbane' fox – elegant, sophisticated, sashaying through the moonlit countryside with food which it will serve to a few foxy friends at a very civilized dinner party. Incidentally, we feel the former Poet Laureate's drawing of a dead chicken does him great credit.

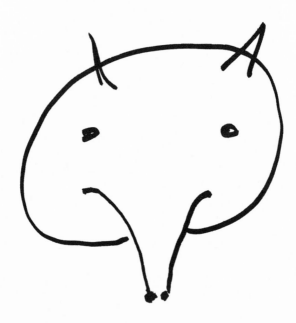

John Julius Norwich, historian and former chairman of the Venice in Peril Fund, may well remember Chad, the star of Second World War graffiti, a perky chap sticking his nose over a wall and saying things like 'Wot, no sugar?' Lord Norwich's fox looks like Chad's urban cousin, sticking his head over the rim of a wheelie bin and saying 'Wot, no taramasalata?'

Writer and publisher Diana Athill – still busy at the age of 97 – gives us an action picture, a moment captured as the fox is poised to attack. It could be a scene from Chaucer's *Nonnes Preestes Tale* with Chauntecleer, deceived by the fox's flattery, about to stand on his toes, flap his wings, close his eyes and crow.

Robert Macfarlane, the award-winning travel writer and creator of this image, says: 'It might be a fox; might be an aardvark . . .' Since our book entitled *Famous People's Aardvarks* is still at an early planning stage, we're going to settle for calling it a fox. Those black triangular eyes are rather sinister.

How clever of children's author Alan Garner to create such a perfectly supercilious-looking fox with just a few strokes of his pen. Those A-shaped eyebrows convey total disdain as Mr Fox looks down the single stroke of his nose. After years of going through dustbins he has no doubt acquired a low opinion of man. Or perhaps he is simply passing judgement on someone's efforts at recycling.

Ronald Blythe

Ronald Blythe's fox, at full stretch and giving an anxious backward glance, is a fine example of what Oscar Wilde called the 'uneatable', and it is clear that the 'unspeakable' are in full pursuit and gaining on him. We'd expect no less from the author of *Akenfield* and other much-loved books on East Anglian country life.

MATT

The cartoonist Matt first offered this drawing for inclusion in a book called *Famous People's Forklift Trucks*. It was rejected, on the grounds that the necessary safety features were not properly displayed. Inexplicably, the drawing was also turned down by *Great British Hen-Houses* magazine, so we agreed to find a place for it here.

As you might expect from the nation's favourite gardener, the spades here are very well executed. The Titchmarsh fox is fluffy and rather glam and its startled expression suggests it may recently have had a facelift. This would make an excellent sign for some cosy little pub, probably named the 'Spade and Vixen', where gardeners go for a well-earned pint or two after a hard day's repotting.

Only a churl would suggest that this drawing of a fox by writer and BBC Radio's *Midweek* presenter Libby Purves is of an ill-natured dachshund by a tree. In any case, a dachshund could never manage that sort of sly, calculating sideways look.

Is it a vixen or a minx? A vixen perhaps – certainly a fox *fatale*. She's just the sort of creation we would expect from the pen of Sue Macartney-Snape, illustrator of the *Telegraph*'s column of 'Social Stereotypes' and a brilliant observer of upper-class types and country gentry. This fox, we suspect, has just bluffed her way into a Hunt Ball and is about to break the heart of the MFH.

This beady, wary, big-eared creature by the eminent biographer Michael Holroyd certainly appears to be related to *Vulpes vulpes* in some way. One theory is that it is an early example of a particular variation of urban fox whose habitat was Bloomsbury in the early part of the last century. It was commonly known as the Virginia wolf.

As Poet Laureate, Carol Ann Duffy has written about contemporary events and issues and refused to be tied down to the traditional Royal milestones. Her drawing is also pleasingly free and original. Here is a fox who knows all the angles, and yet, at the same time, there is something clownish about the tip of that nose.

Booker Prize-winning novelist Kazuo Ishiguro gives us a splendid portrait of Wayne Brush, the disreputable younger brother of that famous and debonair glove puppet Basil. He has been sacked from a series of jobs and has started a number of unsuccessful businesses. Now he has decided to cash in on the family name and become a stand-up comedian. A few gigs on open-mic nights at the lower end of the comedy club circuit have not gone well. At the moment he is filling in as MC at the Foxy Doxy nightspot. Hen parties are his speciality.

First impressions can be deceptive. We took this to be a sketch of an elegant lady's fox fur stole – a clever twist on our theme. However the explanation by the artist and author of *War Horse* is rather grimmer. 'I found this fox on top of a hedgerow on the farm,' he writes. 'Sleeping, I thought. But he was dead.'

A fox, fox-trotting, vulpine, fox-like ...

Alexander McCall Smith

What a well-fed and contented creature we have here from the creator of *The No. 1 Ladies' Detective Agency*. It seems to be fox-trotting through the countryside, away from the scene of the crime. Or if it's an urban fox, then it must be a frequenter of dustbins belonging to the fattest of City fat cats.

Not so much Reynard the Fox, but rather more Pussy Galore – even though that is the wrong Bond film for the distinguished director of *Skyfall*. Just look at those gorgeous liquid eyes and those killer whiskers – and beware.

Isabel Colegate

Famous for her novel *The Shooting Party*, set amid the opulence of a country estate on the eve of the First World War, Isabel Colegate has summoned up a rather elegant creature which looks as if it has been attending obedience classes for foxes, so upright, demure and eager to please. But don't be fooled; as in the novel, there's violence beneath that elegant surface.

Dame Helen Mirren gets right to the point, without senti-
ment. Hers is a ferocious beast, all teeth, snarl and aggression
– in short, a prime suspect. And that chicken is well and
truly spatchcocked.

Some might suggest that this depiction of a fox by the distinguished theatre critic Michael Billington suffers from being under-rehearsed, but we prefer to say that it is thrillingly spontaneous. Still, it's a shame about those ill-fitting dentures.

Wildlife expert and long-time presenter of BBC Television's *Springwatch* Kate Humble must, we think, keep chickens on her farm in the Wye Valley. It's certainly obvious that the fox is not her favourite form of wildlife. Hers is a distinctly malevolent creature with evil eyes. You wouldn't want to have this one peering into your coop.

The fantastic Quentin Blake gives us a jaunty chap with a sackful of poultry and a triumphant glint in his eye. He is obviously on his way back home to his family after a visit to the sheds of those ghastly farmers Boggis, Bunce and Bean, as featured in Quentin's illustrations to Roald Dahl's *Fantastic Mr Fox*.

Some listeners have complained that the plot-lines in *The Archers* have become too racy in recent times. Perhaps we can find a clue to future developments in the work of the actress who plays Shula Hebden Lloyd. Judy Bennett's effort suggests further turmoil with

the arrival of a dodgy poseur from Borchester. He claims to be organizing the Ambridge Literary Festival, but this is merely a cover for mischief of some kind.

In real life, Charles Collingwood is married to Judy Bennett and, in the not-quite-so-real world of *The Archers*, he

has played the part of Brian Aldridge for nearly 40 years, so it is hardly surprising that there is a touch of Aldridge about his fox. It appears to be a bit of a suave charmer, but note that calculating look in the eye – and also those very sharp teeth.

It is entirely appropriate that the author of *Full Tilt: Ireland to India with a Bicycle* (among other cycling adventures) should choose to put her fox on two wheels. The only trouble is, that rear wheel looks to be in need of attention. And the fox (minus a safety helmet) has a rather beaky appearance; if we were being hypercritical we might even say it resembled a chicken. Perish the thought.

WANDA

We asked Michael Palin to do a drawing and he said he couldn't draw. Instead he wrote out a very generous cheque to the Children's Hospital School at Great Ormond Street, which is to receive the proceeds from this book. He had us momentarily foxed, but then we decided to ask our artist B. Lodge to produce this homage to the great man, with a reminder of that 1988 film in which he co-starred. The fox displays a very Palin-ish kindly curiosity, we think.